The Definitive Guide to Cleaning Guns: Rifles, Pistols, Shotguns and Black Powder Rifles

By

Robert Allen Morris

Orchid Springs Publishing, LLC
329 N. Park Ave., Floor 2
Winter Park, FL 32789

Table of Contents

Introduction

Always check and make sure the gun you are about to clean is not loaded. Also, read all safety precautions in the owner's manual. If you no longer have the owner's manual, you can obtain one from the manufacturer, usually online.

In this guide, I mention specific brands of gun cleaning supplies. This is only because my experiences have been limited to these brands. I have not searched further because they have produced the desired results. This is not an endorsement of these brands. Other brands may produce even better results. Readers are encouraged to try various brands of gun cleaning supplies and find what they prefer. Contact information for resources mentioned within this guide is provided in the **Resources** section.

I believe the ideal gun cleaning cloth is medium weight white cotton flannel. It can be purchased in local fabric stores or big box stores like Wal-Mart, or ordered on the internet. Fingerprints contain salt and other chemicals that promote rust. Thus, whenever the metal parts of a gun are touched, this metal should be wiped clean where it was touched. This is especially true after hunting or shooting, where hands may be sweatier than normal. Ideally, the metal should be wiped clean with a lightly oiled cloth within a few hours of being touched. Whenever I go hunting or shooting, at the end of the day I wipe all the exposed metal portions of the gun or guns I used with a piece of cotton flannel cloth coated <u>lightly</u> with Rig or EEZOX. Guns that have the barrel and receiver coated in a camouflage pattern such as Mossy Oak Break-Up at the factory need not be wiped off.

All Non - Black Powder Guns

My favorite rust preventives are rig (rust inhibiting grease) and EEZOX. Rig has been produced since 1935, and is the best rust preventive I know of. Most sporting goods stores carried Rig in the 1950's, 1960's and 1970's, but not now. It can be ordered from Silencio, in Sparks, Nevada. Rig is ideal for coating a cloth to use for wiping fingerprints off of gun metal and for coating a cloth patch to protect a rifle or pistol bore after it has been cleaned.

For larger applications, such as to protect a shotgun bore (not a rifle or pistol bore) after it has been cleaned or for using like a solvent to clean and at the same time lubricate dirty gun parts, EEZOX is ideal, particularly in a spray can. It dries about 10 minutes after application. It can be purchased in most gun stores.

EEZOX should not be used to protect rifle or pistol bores after they have been cleaned. EEZOX can't be wiped out of the bore with a dry cloth and it will destabilize bullets, doubling group sizes. Even firing up to 10 times often will not get all the EEZOX out of a bore enough to restore accuracy. The only way to get it out is to clean the bore with solvent-soaked patches and a bronze bristle brush the same as cleaning after firing rounds through the bore, then remove the solvent from the bore with dry patches. Since there is no rifling or accuracy issue with shotguns, EEZOX is fine to use in shotgun bores.

The cloth used to wipe guns down after use shouldn't be coated too heavily in Rig or EEZOX, otherwise it will attract dirt, and on working parts, powder fouling. Cut a piece of cotton flannel cloth about 5 inches by 5 inches in size. Spray EEZOX on both sides of this piece of cloth to coat it evenly. Then squeeze the cloth between two paper towels to soak up about half the oil on the patch. With Rig, I use my finger to coat one side of the cloth evenly with the grease. Then I roll the cloth between my hands to get it saturated into both sides of the cloth. After this, I open the patch into a flat piece of cloth and put the greasy patch between two paper towels, roll it up tightly and squeeze it to get the paper towels to soak up some of the grease. This soaking up the grease with the paper towels must usually be repeated 3-4 times, changing to fresh paper towels each time, for cloth saturated in Rig in order to get enough grease out for there to be only a light coating.

Avoid getting EEZOX, Rig or any other oil on wooden gun stocks, because this will soften and weaken the wood. Clean the oil off the hand you will touch the stock with when you are putting the gun away, or cover that hand with a cotton glove. You can keep the rig cloth for future use by storing it in a zip lock bag. Cloth saturated with EEZOX is only good for about 10 minutes because the EEZOX dries out, so don't keep it.

For cleaning rifles you'll need a rest to hold it in. The rest should hold the rifle steady while the cleaning rod is worked back and forth and be padded with cloth or rubber to prevent scratching the barrel and stock. It should also cradle the rifle at an angle where the muzzle is lower than the receiver so solvent drains away from the chamber. The one I have is plastic with rubber-coated cradles to hold the gun. It also has a storage area for cleaning equipment, gun parts, etc. It's called the MTM Gun Maintenance Center and is made by the MTM Molded Products Company in Dayton, Ohio. Bass Pro Shops' Outdoor World sells them for about $33.00. The same rest can be used to hold shotgun barrels when cleaning them. It is pictured throughout this guide.

Whenever I disassemble a gun to clean the working parts, I use a cotton flannel cloth coated with EEZOX. It is both a cleaning solvent and rust protector, and more importantly, it dries in about ten minutes. While a small amount of gun oil is needed to lubricate working parts, it is not a good idea to use it for cleaning working parts. That's because gun oil is difficult to dry off from working parts, and if left on, it will attract powder fowling and result in jams and/or misfires, particularly for semi-automatics. If you need something stronger than EEZOX, try Hoppe's No. 9 solvent.

Center Fire Bolt-Action Rifles

When a center fire rifle is fired, powder leaves a residue as it burns, called powder fouling, and the copper jacket on the bullet leaves a residue as it travels down the barrel called copper fouling. These residues build up after every shot, particularly the copper fouling. This buildup of residues will be greatest at the part of the barrel in front of the chamber where the rifling starts, called the throat. Once this buildup gets large enough, say after about 20 shots, it sizes each bullet as it passes it.

Reader's left to right. Pro-Shot Products copper solvent IV, Hoppe's No. 9 powder and lead solvent, EEZOX rust protector, Degreaser spray for getting solvent off of brushes, Rig grease, Dewey bore guide, bronze brush, brass pistol rod also used for cleaning rifle chambers, one piece coated Dewey rod at bottom.

Since the sized bullet no longer exactly fits the bore, an amount of accuracy is lost. Even if this build up is only .002 to .003 inch in thickness, it will reduce accuracy. Properly cleaning the bore is the only way to prevent this buildup of residues and resulting loss of accuracy. If the barrel is not cleaned after firing 20 shots or more, the powder and copper residue will chemically bond and be ironed into a compound harder than the steel it adheres to. Once this happens, it can't be removed without damaging the barrel and accuracy is forever lost.

Cleaning equipment for a center fire bolt-action rifle consists of a rest to hold the rifle, a rod, a slotted tip or a jag to hold the cleaning patch, a bore brush, and a bore guide.

Other cleaning materials include a roll of paper towels, a bottle of Pro-Shot Products copper solvent IV (discussed later), a small bowl to put the solvent in, a plastic cup for draining dirty (waste) solvent into, Rig and possibly EEZOX. A can of degreaser spray will also be needed to remove the copper solvent from the brush before it starts dissolving the bristles. I like the Birchwood Casey brand, which can be purchased at most gun shops, and at Outdoor World. You spray it on, it removes all the solvent and dries in only a few minutes.

The rod should always be one piece, and vinyl, nylon coated, or made of brass, to protect the bore. Brass is softer than the steel a rifle barrel is made of and brass cleaning equipment won't damage the bore if used properly. Also, rod size must be appropriate for the caliber bore being cleaned. For example, a larger rod is required for cleaning a .30 caliber rifle than for cleaning a .22 caliber rifle. The .30 caliber rod won't fit the .22 caliber bore, and if a .22 caliber rod is used for cleaning a .30 caliber, the smaller rod will tend to bow as it's worked and damage the rifling. Top quality cleaning rods will come in different sizes for .17 caliber, .22-.26 caliber, .27 - .338 caliber and .35 caliber and up.

For cleaning rifles, never use two or three piece rods, even if they are coated or made of brass, and never use aluminum or steel rods because all these types of rods will damage the bore and affect accuracy. A three piece rod will cut the bore at the joints in the rod. Aluminum oxide will form on aluminum rods, and like microscopic sandpaper, will scrape the bore with each pass, followed by a loss of accuracy. A steel rod can damage the bore because its steel is not enough softer than the steel the rifle's bore is made from. Bore damage from using these types of rods won't usually be apparent to the naked eye because it's microscopic. But it will affect accuracy.

These three piece, aluminum and steel rods are only made because they're cheaper than one piece coated or brass rods and most hunters don't know that using them will hurt accuracy. For example, a one-piece coated Dewey rod with brass jag and bronze brush is about $35.00. Some sporting goods stores sell a cleaning kit containing one three piece rod that "cleans both rifles and shotguns", gun oil, bore solvent, patches and patch puller all in a wooden box for $19.99. I think it would probably be better to never clean a rifle than subject it to this $19.99 cleaning kit.

Slotted tips and jags should always be made of brass and brushes should have bronze bristles and a brass core, again because this material is softer than the steel the barrel is made from and it won't damage the bore if used properly. A slotted tip holds the cleaning patch in its slot. A jag is a spear-like device that pierces the patch in its center. By piercing the center of the patch, the jag enables the patch to more completely cover the round bore. But the slotted tip enables using a larger patch. My preference is a slotted tip, but more passes through the bore with more patches may be required for a thorough cleaning when using a slotted tip. Most gunsmiths and competition shooters use jags.

The two areas of a rifle barrel that are most critical to its accuracy are where the bullet first contacts the rifling, called the throat, and where the bullet leaves the barrel at the muzzle, called the crown. The reason that a rifle should not be cleaned from the muzzle end is to prevent the cleaning rod from damaging the crown, which would greatly reduce accuracy. When cleaning a rifle from the chamber or breech end, a bore guide should be used to prevent damaging the throat. Bore guides are fitted metal tubes that go in place of the rifle's bolt to enable precisely aligning the rod in the bore. If a bore guide isn't used, the cleaning rod can damage the rifling lands just forward of the chamber in the throat and hurt accuracy. A bore guide also

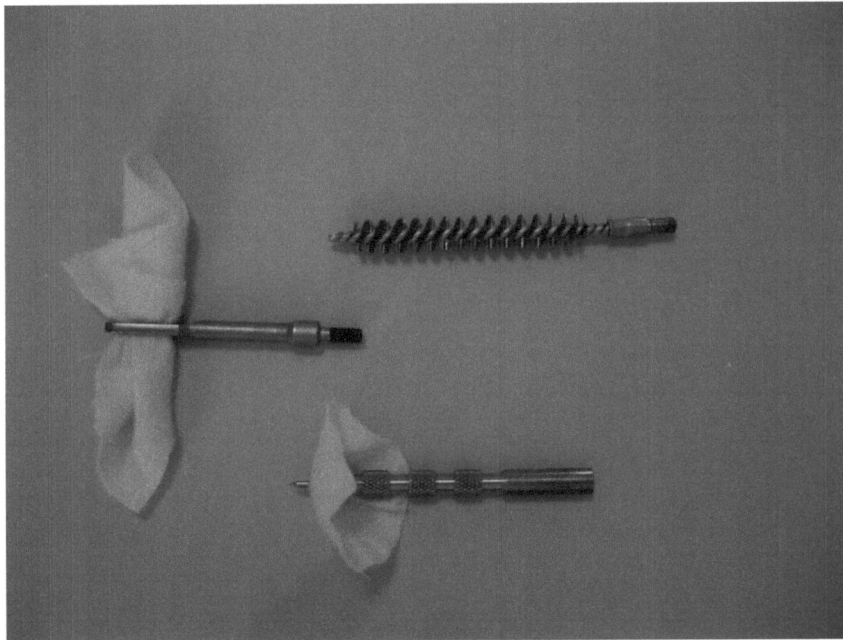

Bronze bristle brush with brass core, slotted tip and jag, with cotton flannel patches.

helps prevent getting solvent in the sensitive trigger mechanism and in the stock bedding. It should have a rubber O-ring on the end that goes in the chamber that seals the chamber completely. Different size bore guides are made to fit different ranges of calibers (.17-.22, .24-.28, .30-.338, etc.) Beware of bore guides where one is supposed to fit all calibers, because it won't and the result will be a poor chamber fit and potentially damaged throat and bore.

Rifle in rest with bore guide properly placed. Note bolt removed and stored in rest compartment under rifle and rod in rest rack.

When a center fire rifle is shot, the bore is fouled from two sources, powder fouling and copper fouling. When a .22 rim fire rifle is fired with short, long or long rifle bullets (which have no copper jacket) or when a shotgun is fired, there's powder and lead fouling, but no copper fowling. Hoppe's No. 9 cleaning solvent, manufactured since the early 1900's, is a good all purpose gun cleaning solvent that removes both powder and lead fouling. It's my choice to remove the lead fowling from .22 rim fires and shotguns. But Hoppe's No. 9 won't remove copper fouling. There are a number of effective copper solvents such as Sweets 7.62, Shooter's Choice, Barnes CR10, Hoppe's Bench rest, etc. These all work, but my favorite solvent to remove copper fowling, and it also effectively removes powder fowling, is Pro-Shot

Copper Solvent IV. It's also the favorite of the U.S. Olympic shooting team. It has no odor and can be used inside, won't damage the bore unless allowed to stay in the bore for several hours, and can be removed with dry patches.

My favorite manufacturer of one piece coated rods, brass cleaning equipment and bore guides is J. Dewey Manufacturing Co. in Oxford, Connecticut. Another good manufacturer of bronze/brass brushes, jags and slotted tips (not rods) is Pro-Shot Products in Taylorville, Illinois. And as mentioned above, Pro-Shot also makes my favorite copper solvent. These cleaning materials and products can be ordered over the telephone from each of these companies. Also, Addison's Gun Shop in Kissimmee, Florida carries both Dewey and Pro-Shot products. Not many other stores carry these products, so don't depend on being able to easily get them if you are away on a hunting trip.

When most rifles leave the factory, they've been test fired once. A coat of rust protecting grease is put on the gun metal and in the bore. This rust preventive was put in the bore without cleaning it after it was shot, leaving the bore a mess. Thus the rifle's bore must be cleaned before it is shot. This cleaning should be as thorough as if the rifle had been shot a number of times, not just a few passes through the bore with an oily patch. This factory rust preventive will stain hands, clothing and gun cases and it was so abundantly applied that it will attract dirt when the gun is being used. Thus, this rust preventive should be wiped off of all exterior metal of the gun, such as the barrel, receiver and outside parts of the bolt. EEZOX is ideal for cleaning this rust preventive off of the exterior metal of the gun, and it leaves behind a less sticky rust preventive that won't stain or attract dirt as much.

I like to put an old clean towel down to clean guns on for two reasons. First, a clean towel prevents dirt from getting on my cleaning rod and its attachments which would ultimately end up in the rifle barrel, and second, it keeps the table or work bench I'm using from stains. To clean the barrel, first put the rifle in the rest. Remove the bolt according to the manufacturer's instructions in the owner's manual and put it in a safe, clean place. The rifle should be positioned upright, just as if you were going to fire it from the rest, and the muzzle should be lower than the receiver, so solvent drains toward the muzzle.

Take an appropriately sized bore guide and place it in the action in place of the bolt. The bore guide's bolt handle should fit down into the notch in the stock just as the rifle's bolt does. This holds the bore guide in place when pulling a cleaning brush back through the bore toward the receiver. Next take several sections of paper towel and fold them into a piece about 3 inches by 5 inches. Put this paper towel under the bore guide at its rear, between the bore guide and the top of the gun stock. The paper towel should cover the area under the bore guide from the entrance to the bore guide to the start of where the rifle's bolt channel begins. This paper towel will soak up solvent that leaks out during cleaning and prevent it from getting on the gun stock and into the action.

Attach the slotted tip or the jag to the cleaning rod and place it next to the gun in its rest. Also lay out the bronze cleaning brush, roll of paper towels, bottle of Pro-Shot Products copper solvent IV, bowl to put the solvent in, plastic cup for draining dirty (waste) solvent into, can of degreaser spray, Rig and EEZOX.

Cut a cotton flannel patch about the size you think is right for the bore. If using a slotted tip, for a .30 caliber that's about 2.5 inches by 2.75 inches. For a 7MM (.284 caliber) it's about 2.25 X 2.25 inches. For a cleaning jag, the patch size will be smaller and should be cut into a round circle to better fit the round bore. Experiment with dry patches until you get the right size. The patch should go through the bore with force, but not enough force to bow the cleaning rod. Once you've got the right patch size, use this as a model to cut 15-20 patches. Keep the model patch to use in the future.

Pour about two ounces of the solvent into the small bowl. Soak a cloth patch in this, squeeze the patch between your fingers to squeeze out enough that it's not dripping with solvent and put it in the slotted tip or on the jag. Push the patch into the bore guide, then through the bore in one smooth motion. This patch will probably be stained black or grey, which is powder fouling. It may also have some blue stain on it, which is copper fouling. Remove the dirty patch and discard it. Then pull the cleaning rod back out of the barrel. Never pull a solvent-soaked patch back from the muzzle to the receiver. Take it off once it goes out the muzzle end. This prevents dragging dirt back through the bore. If you are using a jag the patch can't be pulled back through the bore from the muzzle end because the patch, if properly placed on the jag, will come off rather than go back through the bore.

Continue pushing solvent soaked patches through the bore until they are no longer black. Add more solvent to the bowl as needed. This will take about 4-8 patches, or in some cases, more. Once the patches are no longer black or grey, the powder fouling, which was the black stain on these patches, is now removed. But the bore is not yet cleaned. When the last of this initial series of 4-8 patches is no longer black or grey, remove it, pull the rod back through the bore, and let the solvent-saturated bore soak for 10 minutes. This enables the solvent to work on the copper fouling. Take a paper towel and wipe the solvent off the cleaning rod and off its slotted tip or jag while the barrel is soaking. Also wipe any solvent off the muzzle of the gun and off of any other exterior parts of the gun it may have gotten on. Pro-Shot copper solvent IV may discolor some types of blued gun metal and take the finish off of wooden stocks if left in contact for a prolonged period.

After the barrel has soaked 10 minutes, attach the bronze brush to the cleaning rod. Hold the rod up so the brush is at the bottom, positioned above the plastic waste solvent cup. Then drizzle solvent slowly down the length of the brush so it runs off into the waste solvent cup (not the bowl with clean solvent in it) and completely coats the brush. Next push the brush into the bore guide and on through the bore. Unlike with patches, the brush should also be pulled back through the bore from muzzle to receiver. This improves its cleaning action and it won't pull dirt back through the bore like patches will. This brushing process should be done in two smooth, relatively quick motions, push it through the borer, then pull it back through the bore and out the bore guide. Do this three times, for a total of six passes with the brush through the bore. Never reverse a bore brush inside the barrel. Always push it out the muzzle end before pulling it back through the bore.

Next, take the brush, still attached to the cleaning rod, outside and spray the brush with the degreaser to remove the solvent. Then use a paper towel to clean the solvent off the rod. Remove the brush, attach the tip or jag, and push a solvent-soaked patch through the bore. Remember to remove the patch at the muzzle, don't pull it back through the bore like you did the brush. The patch will probably have blue stain on it, indicating the removal of copper fouling. Wipe any solvent off the muzzle of the gun with a paper towel and off the cleaning rod and slotted tip or jag. Let the bore soak again for 10 minutes, then repeat the procedure, first brushing three times (six passes) followed by pushing a solvent-soaked patch through the bore. Repeat the brushing and patching with 10 minute intervals until a second patch used without brushing with the bronze bristle brush has no stain. Try this second patch after four times of brushing and patching. If it is still stained, try again after four times of brushing and patching. You may have to cut more patches. The reason for testing the bore to see if it is clean after a patch has been passed through rather than after the brush is that some of the blue stain is from the brass bristle brush. Once the patch is simply white (the color of the cloth if you use white cotton flannel) and has no stain, the bore is clean. If not, continue the brushing and patching procedure until it is clean. Once the bore is cleaned, dry the muzzle off with a paper towel, dry the cleaning rod and tip or jag, then push four clean dry patches through the bore to dry it out.

The chamber needs to be cleaned next, but in rifles this is simple and easy because no copper fouling and very little powder fouling gets in the chamber. However, what's there should be cleaned. It should also be protected with rust preventive because cartridges you load into the gun have your fingerprints or sometimes your sweat on them and can promote rust in the chamber if it's not protected. You can use the cleaning rod you cleaned the rifle with, but a short 9-12 inch long pistol rod is easier to use. This pistol rod should also be coated or made of brass like the rifle rod, and they can also be purchased from Dewey Manufacturing. Attach a brass slotted tip, not a jag, to the rod. Cut a piece of flannel patch several times larger than the patches cut for the bore. Attach this larger patch to the pistol rod and experiment by pushing it into and out of the chamber, then cutting it down or trying a larger patch to find out what gives a snug fit in the chamber. This experimenting will also dry out any solvent that may have gotten in the chamber. Once you've determined the right size for a chamber patch, cut one and saturate it with rig. I do this by spreading rig on one side of the patch and rolling it between my fingers to saturate the patch. Dry about half of the rig off the patch by squeezing it between two pieces of paper towel, changing to new paper towel several times until the patch is slightly greasy to the touch, but not saturated. Then pass this patch in and out of the chamber three or four times.

Now it's time to protect the clean, dry bore from rust. Saturate a patch with Rig. Then use paper towels to dry about a third of the grease from the patch. This patch for protecting the bore should be greasier than the patch for the chamber and greasier than the cloth you use to wipe up the exterior metal of the rifle. Then push this patch through the bore three or four times to protect the bore. Remove the paper towels and rod guide, and use a paper towel to wipe off any solvent that got on the gun. Use a cotton flannel cloth about 5 inches by 5 inches lightly coated with Rig or EEZOX to wipe off the bolt face, the bolt, the area in front of the chamber, down in the magazine, and all exposed metal parts of the rifle. The rifle is now cleaned and ready to put away. When you get ready to shoot it at the range or go hunting with it, before shooting it, run three or four dry patches through the bore to remove the Rig.

Discard any solvent left in the bowl. Do not keep it because soaking the patches in it made it un-storable. Obviously the waste solvent that dripped off the bronze brushes into the plastic cup is contaminated and must be discarded.

The bolt and trigger mechanism should be disassembled and cleaned, but only after about every 50 shots. The manual that came with the rifle will probably have instructions about how to do this. But I take it to a gunsmith rather than attempt it myself. It's rare to shoot a hunting rifle more than 50 times in less than say 5 years, so I would rather pay the relatively small cost to have a capable gunsmith do this than try what would be an unfamiliar process myself and potentially damage an expensive hunting rifle.

Sometime you may be in a situation where your rifle bore needs to be cleaned and you don't have or can't find a place to buy the proper cleaning equipment. For example, away on a hunt and the rifle muzzle was jammed in the dirt or the rifle fell in a lake or stream. Don't go buy or borrow an improper cleaning kit that may damage the bore. If the bore is clogged with dirt, use a wooden stick to unclog it. Then obtain a stout piece of string about 36 inches long. 20 pound test fishing line would be ideal. Attach a small weight to one end of the line. A small lead sinker would be ideal but a hair pin also works. Tie a cleaning patch to the other end of the string. Put a paper towel or piece of cloth in the action to prevent getting oil or solvent in it.

Coat the patch in solvent, or oil if that's all you have, drop the weighted end of the string through the chamber and out the muzzle, then pull the patch through. Repeat with additional patches until the bore is clean. If solvent is used, dry out the solvent with dry patches and protect the bore with a lightly oiled patch. Remove this oil with dry patches before firing the rifle. You can't brush the bore, but unless the rifle has been fired more than 20 times, it won't need brushing anyway. In anticipation of a problem like this, I carry an Otis plastic-coated cable flex rod with slotted tip (discussed later), cotton flannel patches cut to the right size, bronze brush, bore guide, solvent and Rig on hunting trips. These cleaning materials take up very little space and pack conveniently in my suitcase.

The most important bore cleaning for a new rifle is the first few times it is cleaned. These, more than any other cleanings, will set the basis for the future accuracy of this rifle. When barrels are cut and rifled, microscopic machining marks are left in the bore. Some cheaper barrels have a lot of machining marks, while other, more expensive barrels have fewer marks. These marks create a rough bore that shaves off tiny bits of copper from bullet jackets when the bullets are shot through the bore. This fouls the bore more quickly and hampers accuracy. Most of these machining marks can be smoothed out by simply shooting and cleaning the rifle, or "breaking in" the barrel. Fired bullets traveling down a clean barrel cause enough pressure and friction to clear out machining marks. The important thing is that the barrel is clean so that the passing bullet can work directly against the bore. So the break-in procedure is a process of cleaning and firing.

Different rifle barrels have different degrees of roughness, so the amount of shooting and cleaning required will vary by barrel. Also, the process described here is for hunting rifles. Bench rest competition barrels will require much more breaking in. My rule of thumb for a new hunting rifle barrel is to clean the bore as described previously after each of the first three shots. You can skip the last cleaning step, where you put a light coat of Rig to rust-protect the bore, until you are finished shooting for the day. Thus after each cleaning, you will be shooting from a clean dry bore. Do this shooting and cleaning in one shooting session at the range, preferably when you are sighting in the new rifle. Once you've cleaned the bore after each of the first three shots, clean the bore after each three shots in a row for the next 30 shots. This should smooth the bore enough to significantly reduce copper fouling and improve accuracy.

Once you are into the cleaning after each three shots process, you don't need to stay at the range and shoot 30 times in one day unless you want to. Just keep track of the number of shots while sighting in, practicing and hunting, and remember to clean after every three shots, until you reach a total of 24 shots. After this, the bore should be cleaning up easier, requiring fewer solvent patches to get it clean. If not, continue another 12 rounds of cleaning after every three rounds. Once the bore is smoothed somewhat from this process, it should only require cleaning after about every 20 rounds are fired through it, or if fewer rounds have been fired, every 3-4 months. If a dirty bore sits too long, the copper and powder fouling will begin to adhere to the metal in the barrel.

When shooting a center fire rifle at the range or when practicing, it's important not to let the barrel get too hot. If it does, the build-up of copper fouling at the throat will start to weld to the barrel, hurting accuracy and making it much more difficult to clean. My rule of thumb is to let the barrel cool for about 15-20 minutes after every three shots. But this cooling time will vary on hot and cold days. It's cooled enough when the barrel is barely warm to the touch. I don't impose this rule when hunting for two reasons. First, it's rare to get more than three shots in rapid succession at game. And second, shooting more than three times in rapid succession at an animal will be rare enough that it won't damage the barrel.

Center Fire Lever Actions and Semi-Automatic Rifles

While some brands of lever actions and semi-automatics have a take-down feature that enables them to be cleaned from the breech end, many do not. Thus, they must be cleaned from the muzzle end. If a cleaning rod is used, even a one-piece coated rod, cleaning a rifle from the muzzle can ultimately damage the crown and reduce accuracy.

Otis Technology, Inc. offers a solution. Their products can be purchased at many gun shops, or ordered directly from Otis Technology, Inc. in Lyons Falls, New York. Otis flex rods are pieces of steel cable covered with plastic offered in eight different lengths ranging from 8 inches long for short handguns up to 40 inches long for rifles. They also make a six-inch long flex rod for cleaning chambers. Flex rods come in two thicknesses, one for .22 and .17 calibers, and another for all calibers larger than this. On one end is a threaded brass piece that a slotted tip or bronze cleaning brush can be screwed into. On the other end is a brass piece with a hole through it that a small brass pull pin, called a T-handle, can be inserted in to enable pulling the cable through the bore with a cleaning patch or brush attached.

The brass slotted tips made by Otis Technologies work best on their flex rods because they form a more uniform fit between the slotted tip and its receptacle. Otis also makes bronze brushes with a brass core for their flex rods. These are shorter than traditional bronze brushes made for cleaning bolt-action rifles, and should be used with Otis flex rods because they fit better into the relatively short space in front of the chambers of lever-action and semi-automatic rifles. Other brushes such as those made by Pro-Shot products and Dewey will fit Otis flex rods, but may be too long to fit into semi-automatic and lever action rifles. These longer brushes can be used when Otis flex rods are used to clean bolt-actions, like on a hunting trip or for .22 rim fire bolt actions.

If an Otis brush will not fit into the space in the action of the rifle you are cleaning, the brush can be cut shorter, or possibly this make of rifle has a take-down feature that enables removing the barrel for cleaning. If this won't work, you can either brush it from the muzzle and potentially reduce accuracy, or take the gun to a gunsmith for disassembly and cleaning. The Otis flex rod enables cleaning a semi-automatic , lever action or pump rifle from the breech end. Simply push the end of the flex rod opposite from the slotted tip from the breech out through the muzzle. Then put a patch in the slotted tip and pull it through the bore. The patch used on an Otis flex rod will be larger than the one used with a standard cleaning rod because the patch is being pulled through the bore rather than pushed, thus it has no rod to wrap around. You may have to use the T-handle to give enough leverage to pull the patch through. When it is time to brush the bore, follow the same procedure used for pulling patches through the bore with a bronze brush screwed onto the end of the flex rod to pull it through the bore.

Use the same bore cleaning procedure with the Otis flex rod as for bolt-action rifles with the traditional cleaning rod. When a bolt-action is cleaned with a brush, the brush is pushed and pulled through the bore three times, for a total of six passes, between cleaning with patches. This gets cumbersome with a flex rod where the brush can only be pulled through the bore, so I pull the brush through the bore three times, for a total of three passes, in between cleanings with patches. Also, when the

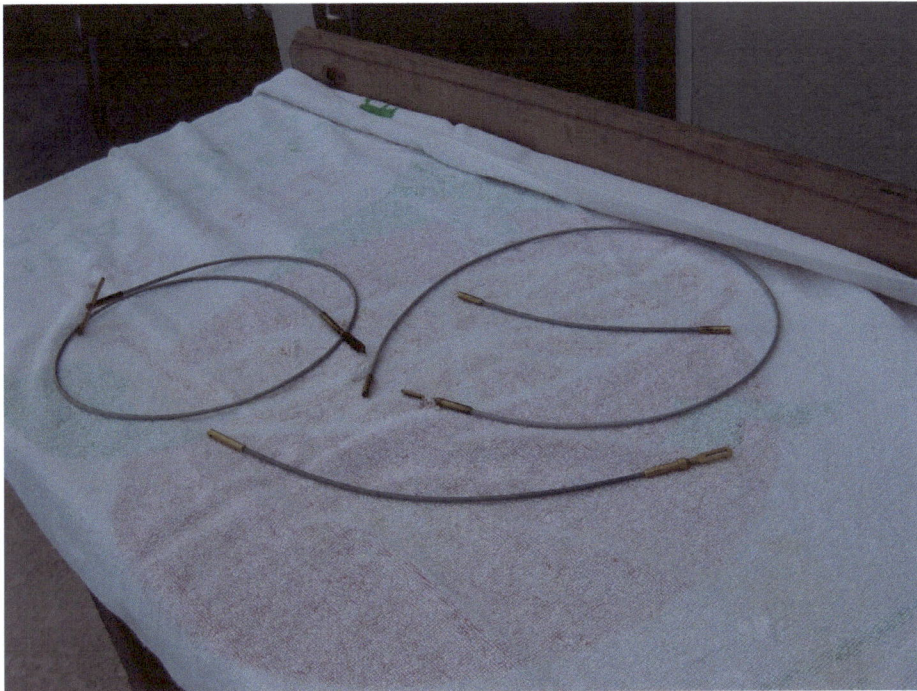

Otis flex rods. Note T-handle on flex rod at the left to aid in pulling on flex rod with bronze brush.

brush is just leaving the chamber and entering the bore, twist it two or three turns by twisting the flex rod with the T-handle. Since the brush can't be scrubbed back and forth with a flex rod like it can with a traditional rod, this twisting helps clean the throat of the bore. A bore guide can't be used, so put some absorbent cloth in the open action just beneath the chamber where the patch enters the bore to catch drips of solvent. When this cloth becomes wet, put another dry cloth in its place. Finish the same as in cleaning a bolt-action, by using several patches to dry the solvent out of the bore, then pulling a patch lightly coated with Rig through the bore three or four times to protect it from rust.

To clean the chamber, use the six inch flex rod and insert a patch into the chamber by pushing on the slotted tip and flex rod just behind the slotted tip. Once the patch is in the chamber, insert the T-bar into the other end of the rod and turn the patch in the chamber by turning the flex rod. Experiment to find the correct size patch. Once the correct size is determined, cut a patch this size. Coat lightly with rig and clean the chamber by inserting the patch and twisting it.

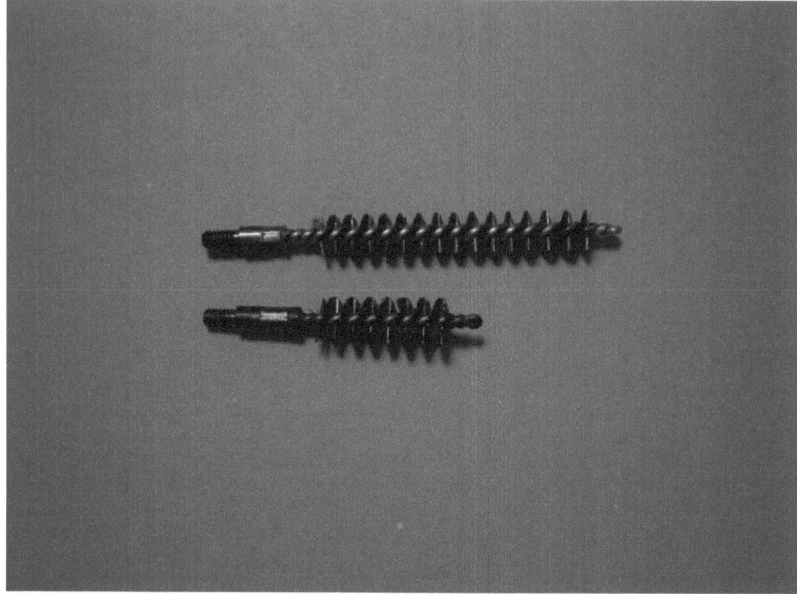

**Typical .30 caliber rifle bronze brush at top and shorter
Bronze brush for Otis flex rod beneath.**

An Otis flex rod with slotted tip, bronze brush and patches cut to fit will all fit into a small zip lock bag. As was mentioned earlier, it makes an ideal portable cleaning kit for taking on hunting trips even if bolt-action rifles will be used.

The action of a semi-automatic or lever action rifle should be taken apart after about every 50 shots and cleaned in order to keep the action functioning smoothly. The owner's manual will provide instructions about how to disassemble the gun. For me, it is several years before I will shoot a center fire rifle 50 times, so I am never familiar with the process of disassembling them. Thus, I take them to a gunsmith for this cleaning.

Assault Rifles

This is for the AR 15, which can be easily dissembled (field stripped) so the barrel and bolt can be removed for cleaning. Following the instructions in the owner's manual, pull the rear take down pin out until it comes to a stop. Pivot the lower receiver down and away from the upper receiver and barrel. Release the charge handle and take out the bolt carrier assembly. Slide the front pivot pin to the side and separate the upper and lower part of the rifle. Put the upper part of the rifle (the chamber and barrel) in the rest. Insert an assault rifle bore guide through the receiver and into the chamber. At this point, cleaning the barrel is the same as for a bolt action rifle, patching and brushing until the solvent-soaked patches are clean, drying the solvent out of the barrel with several patches, then following with a patch containing Rig or gun oil to prevent rust. Clean the chamber the same as instructed for a bolt action. Next, following the instructions in the owner's manual, remove the firing pin from the bolt carrier assembly. Remove the bolt cam and pull the bolt out. Press out the pivot pin and remove the extractor. Soak the small parts from the bolt and bolt carrier assembly in Hoppe's No. 9 solvent. Use a bronze wire brush to clean fouling off of the solvent-soaked parts. Clean out the inside of the gas key on the bolt carrier with a Q-tip. Wipe all the parts dry, then coat a cloth with EEZOX and wipe the parts to prevent rust. Put a couple of drops of gun oil at the back of the bolt and on the gas ring. Then reassemble the rifle and put it away.

Rim Fire Rifles

This includes the .22 long rifle, the .22 magnum, the .17 HMR and the .17 Mach 2. It does not include center fire .22 caliber rifles like the .223, the .22-250, the .220 Swift, etc. The cleaning methods for center fire rifles described previously apply to these center fire .22 calibers. All of these rim fire rifles but the .22 long rifle use copper jacketed bullets and should be cleaned with Pro Shot Copper Solvent IV. The .22 long rifle can be cleaned with Hoppe's No. 9 solvent.

Hoppe's No. 9 solvent is sold in most gun stores, including Wal-Mart and Outdoor World. The large 16 ounce bottle is a much better buy than the smaller 4 and 2 ounce bottles, which are not even enough to clean a shotgun once. Hoppe's No. 9 is manufactured by Bushnell Outdoor Products located in Overland Park, Kansas

The cartridge case is the same as the bullet diameter for .22 caliber rim fires, so a bore guide can't be used. Consequently, I use an Otis flex rod for cleaning .22 rim fire rifles, whether they are bolt action, lever action or semi-automatic.

The .22 long rifle can be cleaned with Hoppe's No. 9 cleaning solvent and an Otis flex rod with slotted tip and bronze brush. Simply substitute it for the Pro-Shot Copper Solvent IV that is used to clean center fire rifles. Powder and lead fouling will be black, not blue like the copper fouling removed with copper solvent IV. Also, when cleaning with Hoppe's No.9, there's no need to let the bore soak between brushings. Simply alternate brushing and pulling a solvent-soaked patch through the bore until the patch comes out light grey instead of black. Then follow with another solvent-soaked patch without brushing. If this solvent-soaked patch is not clean, continue brushing and patching until the second solvent-soaked patch after brushing is clean. If this second solvent-soaked patch is clean, dry the bore with several patches, then lightly coat it with Rig to protect it from rust.

The .17 HMR and the .17 Mach 2 have cartridge cases larger than the bullet diameter, thus a bore guide can be used for cleaning, and should be if a cleaning rod is used. Dewey makes both one piece rods and bore guides for the .17 caliber rim fires. However, an Otis flex rod and attachments will suffice. That's what I prefer for cleaning this tiny delicate bore. If you use a cleaning rod, use a jag and not a slotted tip. The bore is too small for a patch in a slotted tip to provide adequate coverage. The patch will be very small, smaller than a dime. Just experiment to find the right size. Start too small and go up so you don't get a patch stuck in the bore, since it can't be pulled backward with a jag. Clean with Pro-Shot copper Solvent IV, the same as for a center fire rifle, and use Rig as a rust preventive after cleaning.

<u>Always clean new guns thoroughly, particularly the barrel, before shooting them the first time.</u> The .22 long rifle does not require any barrel break in since it uses a lead bullet, and the bore will only need to be cleaned about every 100 shots. The bore can also be left dirty for up to a year and still be cleaned easily. The other rim fires use jacketed bullets, though at a slower velocity than most center fire rifles, thus a break-in procedure similar to that used for center fire rifles should be used for these rim fires. For these jacketed rim fires, skip the first cleaning process of cleaning after every round for the first five shots and instead, clean after every three rounds for the first 33 shots. However, once the bore is broke in, cleaning should only be required about every 50 rounds. For rim fire rifles that fire jacketed bullets, don't leave the bore dirty for more than three months, no matter how few times it has been fired.

The actions of semi-automatic and lever-action .22 rifles should be cleaned after about every 200 shots. Follow the instructions in the owner's manual for disassembly.

Handguns

The two main types of handguns are revolvers and semi-automatics. There are also break-open single shot and bolt-action handguns, but these are specialty guns for big game hunting.

A rest to hold the handgun is not needed. Simply lay out a large towel to work on. For copper jacketed bullets, Pro-Shot copper solvent IV should be used, and for lead bullets, Hoppe's No. 9 can be used. The process to clean a center fire pistol is the same as that to clean a center fire rifle, patching and brushing with solvent until the bore is clean, drying the solvent out of the bore and leaving a light coat of rust-inhibiting grease on the bore. For .22 caliber rim fire handguns, the cleaning process is the same as for .22 rim fire rifles.

For cleaning semi-automatics, a 9-12 inch coated or brass rod should be used. Dewey makes these. Disassemble the pistol according to the manufacturer's instructions in the owner's manual. Remove the barrel and clean it from the breach end, the same as a center fire rifle is cleaned, except without a bore guide. Because the diameter of the cartridge case and bullet for handguns is the same, the diameter of the chamber and bore are the same. Thus a bore guide can't be used and isn't needed. Use a cloth coated lightly with EEZOX or Rig to wipe the dirt and powder residue off of working parts. If the working parts are heavily coated with residue, you may want to use a cloth saturated with Hoppe's No. 9 solvent and a bronze bristle brush to remove stubborn deposits. Dewey makes a bronze gun brush that looks like a tooth brush but has bronze bristles that's ideal for this type of cleaning. It costs about $2.00. Dry off the solvent, and follow with a cloth coated lightly with Rig or EEZOX.

Colt 1911 Gold Cup Match

Since disassembly and assembly of virtually all 1911 semi-automatic handguns is the same, I will describe it here for my Colt Gold Cup. **Disassembly:** Be sure pistol is unloaded and remove the magazine. With muzzle pointed upward, rest pistol on heel of butt on a table or bench. Push slide back about ¼ inch, press down on recoil spring plug (located just below muzzle) and at the same time, using bushing wrench, rotate barrel bushing clockwise about ¼ turn; this will free plug and recoil spring. Keep pressure on plug to prevent it being ejected by the spring, then allow plug and spring to gradually extend out of the slide. Rotate plug counterclockwise and remove from spring. Cock hammer by pulling back on hammer spur. Pull slide to rear until lug on slide stop is opposite disassembly notch and push rounded end of pin of slide stop (on right of receiver) inward and through receiver to disengage slide stop from slide. Lift out slide stop. Pull receiver to rear and off of slide. Lift recoil springs and guide and pull them rearward out of slide. Turn barrel bushing counterclockwise, push barrel bushing forward until bushing is clear of slide, then remove bushing from barrel. Push link forward and remove barrel from front of slide.

Assembly: With slide upside down and barrel link forward, assemble barrel into slide. Place barrel bushing over muzzle of barrel and into slide until it is flush with the face of the slide. Turn bushing clockwise as far as it will go. Place the recoil guide into the recoil springs so that the closed end of the springs are up against the collar of the guide. Assemble the recoil springs into the guide by pushing the open end of the springs through the slide from the rear. Position the arched portion of the recoil spring guide over the outside surface of the barrel. Cock the hammer. Look at the top of the receiver and make sure the plunger lever is down (forward), tip the receiver forward to keep it down as you run the slide onto the receiver. Look through the slide stop hole in the side of the receiver. Move the slide along the receiver until you see the hole in the barrel link line up with the hole in the side of the receiver. Insert the slide stop through the hole until it is almost home. Continue pushing the slide rearward until the disassembly notch lines up with the rear part of the slide stop. Now push the slide stop up and in against the slide stop plunger until the slide stop is fully home. Rest pistol on table or bench with muzzle pointing upward. Push slide back about ¼ inch, press down on recoil spring plug, compressing the recoil spring into the slide until the plug is fully home, then rotate the barrel bushing. Align the arched part of the bushing so that it straddles the recoil spring plug and locks it in place. After assembling the pistol, exercise the slide a few times by pulling it fully rearward and allowing it to slam forward on an empty chamber. Open the slide and lock it open. Then look in the ejection port to ensure that the firing pin is not sticking forward through the hole in the middle of the breech face. You should not be able to see the firing pin. If you do find the firing pin sticking forward, or if at any time your pistol discharges when you close the slide, take or send your pistol to a Colt Authorized Repair Service Station or return it to the factory.

Use the Otis flex rod with slotted tip and bronze pistol brushes to clean the barrel of revolvers from the breach end. Swing the cylinder open on a double action to clean it. Remove the cylinder on a single-action according to instructions in the owner's manual to clean it. The cartridge chambers in the cylinder of a revolver will collect copper and/or lead fouling at the front of the chamber where the bullet contacts it before entering the barrel. Use a brass or coated Dewey pistol rod to clean these cartridge chambers in the cylinder. Clean them the same as the bore, with solvent-soaked patches and a bronze brush. Clean them from the breech end, where the cartridge is loaded into the cylinder. Use Rig as a rust preventive for both bores and cylinders after cleaning. Use a cloth with Rig or EEZOX to clean the powder residue off of all working parts.

Handgun bullets travel at only about 30-50% of the velocity of center fire rifle bullets and they are short range weapons, not designed for precision long-range accuracy like center fire rifles. Thus, handgun barrels do not need to be broke in like rifle barrels. And since they fire bullets at much lower velocity, they don't need to be cleaned as often. <u>Always clean a new gun before shooting it to get out the gunk from the test firing and rust protecting grease.</u> After this, cleaning new handguns after the first 25 rounds should suffice, then after every 100 rounds. Don't leave a handgun bore un-cleaned for more than four months, no matter how few times it has been fired.

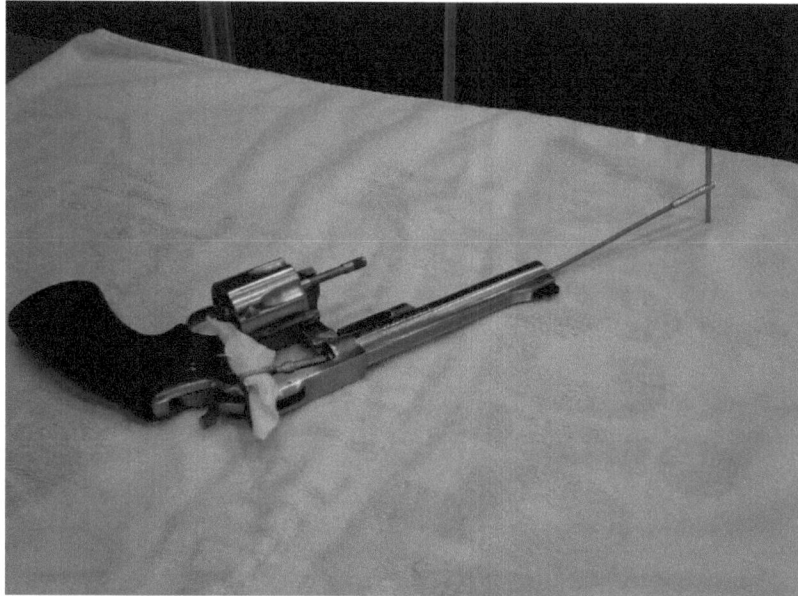

Shotguns

Shotguns have smooth bores, thus they do not need to be cleaned as often as rifles and pistols. Since they fire lead pellets, Hoppe's No. 9 solvent can be used to clean the bore (and the action). Also, a three piece aluminum rod with plastic or aluminum slotted tip is okay for cleaning shotguns, since there's no rifling or accuracy to worry about. These can be purchased at Wal-Mart, Outdoor World, and a number of other stores. I still like to use bronze brushes with brass cores though, ideally those made by Dewey or Pro-Shot Products. There is a different size shotgun brush for each gauge. I like to have one rod for the slotted tip and another for the bronze brush to save time changing from the slotted tip to the bronze brush. Also, a chamber brush may be needed. This is a bronze brush, larger than the brushes used to clean the bore, attached to a rod about 7-8 inches long with a handle. It can be purchased in most gun shops or ordered from Pro-Shot Products. Be sure and get the correct size chamber brush for the gauge shotgun you will be cleaning.

The primary objective for cleaning a shotgun is to keep the action clean enough to function properly, although the bore should be cleaned whenever the gun is cleaned. <u>Always thoroughly clean a new shotgun before shooting it the first time.</u> Over-under and side-by-side double barrels and single barrels have fewer working parts than pumps and semi-automatics. Thus they don't require cleaning as frequently. Cleaning these types of shotguns every 300 rounds should be sufficient. Pump actions, operated manually, and recoil operated semi-automatics, such as those made by Benelli, should be cleaned every 300 rounds. Gas operated semi-automatics (Browning, Remington, Beretta and others) should be cleaned every 100 rounds, or the action may begin to jam. A shotgun that has been fired, no matter how few times, should not be left un-cleaned for more than a year.

Shotgun barrel dissembled from stock and receiver for cleaning and placed in rest. Short chamber rod and brush, rod with slotted tip and rod with bronze brush.

Assemble all the cleaning accessories on an old towel on a work bench in a well-ventilated area. Unlike Pro-Shot Products Copper Solvent IV, Hoppe's No. 9 has a very pungent odor and probably should be used outside. Cleaning equipment will consist of one cleaning rod with a slotted tip, another cleaning rod with a bronze brush of the correct size as the shotgun gauge you're cleaning, a chamber brush attached to a chamber-cleaning rod, cotton flannel for patches and cleaning cloths, a small bowl to put Hoppe's cleaning solvent in, a plastic cup to collect dirty waste-solvent, and a roll of paper towels.

Remove the barrel from the stock and receiver according to the instructions in the owner's manual. Leave the screw-in choke tube in place so it can be cleaned with the barrel. When the choke tubes are cleaned separately, the choke tube can be removed from the barrel to clean the part of the barrel covered by the choke tube, which will be described later. Place the barrel in the same rest that was used to hold the rifle, with the breech end higher than the muzzle so solvent drains toward the muzzle. Experiment with different patches to get one that fits the bore gauge you are cleaning. It should be a tight fit but not too tight, so the patch will go through the bore in one smooth motion. Cut 15 patches this size from the cotton flannel.

Pour about 4 ounces of Hoppe's solvent into the bowl, saturate a patch in the solvent and squeeze the patch out back in the bowl holding clean solvent enough that it isn't dripping. Solvent squeezed from a clean patch will not reduce the effectiveness of solvent held in the bowl, but this solvent should not be returned to its original container. Insert the patch into the slotted tip on the rod and push it through the barrel and out the muzzle. Then pull it back through to the breech and out the chamber. This is two passes through the bore with this patch. Get a clean patch, saturate it with solvent and repeat this procedure. Continue cleaning the bore with solvent-soaked patches until the patches only have a light grey stain. This has removed the powder fouling.

Get the rod with the bronze brush and pour solvent over it from the end where it is attached to the rod, holding the rod in a vertical position with the brush at the bottom to enable the solvent to drizzle down the length of the brush and saturate it. The solvent that drips off the end of the brush should be caught in the plastic waste solvent cup, not back in the bowl holding clean solvent because solvent that is poured over a bronze brush will chemically contaminate clean solvent. Push this solvent-soaked brush through the bore and out the muzzle, then pull it back through to the breech and out the chamber. Push and pull this brush through the bore three times, for a total of six passes through the bore.

Follow this with a solvent-soaked patch, followed by another three times, or six passes, with a solvent soaked brush. Add more solvent to the bowl as needed. Continue this brushing and patching until the patch is light grey rather than black. To check, follow the first light grey patch with another solvent-soaked patch rather than brushing. If it's clean, the bore is clean. Dry the solvent off the muzzle and the chamber end of the barrel with a paper towel. Dry the solvent out of the bore using three dry patches, making two passes (in and out once) through the bore with the first two patches, and four passes (in and out twice) with the third patch. Lift the barrel and look through it. It should have a mirror-like shine. If you notice streaks, continue cleaning with solvent-soaked patches, followed by brushing until the streaks are no longer visible from a dry barrel.

If there are streaks or visible patches in the chamber when looking through the clean, dry barrel, it will need to be cleaned separately. These streaks in the chamber are probably melted plastic from shotgun shells. Saturate a patch with solvent and push it through the bore and out the muzzle, then pull it back through and out the chamber end. Attach the chamber brush to the short chamber cleaning rod and saturate the chamber brush with solvent. Push the chamber brush into the chamber so it goes in the full length of the chamber, which will be 2 ¾ to 3 ½ inches, depending on the shotgun you are cleaning. Work the chamber brush in and out of the chamber with a scrubbing motion four or five times. Saturate a patch with solvent and work it in and out of the chamber several times.

Then use a dry patch to dry the solvent out of the chamber (not the entire barrel). Hold the barrel up to the light and look through it. If the streaks are not removed, clean the chamber again, first with a patch saturated in solvent, then with the chamber brush. When a dry chamber shows no more streaks, saturate another patch with solvent and push it through the bore and out the muzzle, then pull it back through the bore and out the chamber. This removes any dirty solvent that may have gotten in the bore forward of the chamber while cleaning the chamber.

Take this same solvent-soaked patch (which should be relatively clean) and clean any dirt or powder residue off the exposed outside parts of the barrel, muzzle, and chamber end of the barrel. On semi-automatics, be sure and clean the gas bracket under the barrel, and find the hole in the barrel that releases gas to operate the mechanism and use a tooth pick to be sure it is clear of residue. For over-under, double and single barrel shotguns (break-open guns), be sure and clean the ejectors. Also, the exterior part of the barrel where shells are loaded into the chamber of break-open guns often gets stained black. You may need to use a Dewey bronze gun brush and solvent to clean this.

For guns with ported barrels, clean over the port holes with this solvent patch. Dry the solvent off these outside parts of the barrel with a dry patch. Now dry the bore by pushing and pulling three dry patches each through the bore and out the muzzle, then back through the bore and out the chamber. Push and pull the third dry patch through the bore twice (four passes). Spray EEZOX liberally on both sides of a clean patch. Use a paper towel to get about a third of the EEZOX off the patch. Then push and pull this patch through the bore three times to protect it from rust.

Take the patch you just used to protect the bore from rust and wipe the dirt and powder residue off all exposed parts of the action and receiver. See the owner's manual for instructions on how to clean the gun's working parts and for definitions of some of the terms used here. Q-tip swabs with EEZOX sprayed on the tip make handy cleaning aids that get into small nooks and crannies to help clean dirty parts. For a gas operated semi-automatic there will be considerable amounts of powder residue on and around the gas piston and its ports and sleeve, and on the outside of the magazine tube that should all be cleaned off. Also clean the bolt face that contacts the shell, and clean the chamber in the receiver on both semi-automatics and pumps. For pumps, be sure and clean the sleeve the pump operates on and the slides or rails. When clean, the slides should be left with a <u>very</u> light application of Rig or gun oil. For break-open guns, clean the lock and area around it, including the inside of the receiver box. A very light application of Rig should be left on the hinge area of break-open guns where the receiver contacts the hinge pin on the barrel and on both sides of the locking lug.

Coat another patch lightly with EEZOX and wipe down the exterior parts of the barrel that you dried off after cleaning with solvent. Assemble the gun, and use this patch with EEZOX to wipe off all exposed metal. The shotgun is now ready to put away.

The choke tubes for a shotgun should be cleaned with solvent-soaked patches and bronze brush, the same as the barrel. The choke tube in the barrel will be cleaned when the barrel is cleaned. The other choke tubes, the ones that were used, only need cleaning every other time the barrel is cleaned. Whenever the choke tubes are cleaned, also remove the choke tube that is in the barrel so the area where the choke tube was will be cleaned when the barrel is being cleaned. Before starting the barrel cleaning procedure, take a dry patch and use your little finger with the patch to wipe the grease off the threads in the barrel where the choke tube was. A q-tip can also be used. Then clean and rust-protect the barrel, including the area where the choke tube was, as described above.

To clean the choke tubes, saturate a patch in Hoppe's No. 9 solvent and clean off the exterior of each of the choke tubes, including the threads. Next, put a plastic slotted tip on the short chamber cleaning rod and put a solvent-soaked patch in the slotted tip. Run this solvent-soaked patch in and out through each of the choke tubes. Attach a bronze bore brush (not a chamber brush) to the chamber rod and saturate the brush with solvent. Run this solvent-soaked brush in and out of each of the choke tubes twice. Follow with a solvent-soaked patch in and out of each choke tube.

Run a dry patch in and out of each choke tube to dry out the solvent. Change to a new dry patch after every two choke tubes. Inspect the interior of each choke tube. If it's still dirty, repeat this procedure until it's clean. When it's clean, run a patch lightly coated with EEZOX in and out of each choke tube to protect them from rust. Then use a little Rig on your fingers to lightly lubricate the threads on each of the choke tubes. Screw one of the choke tubes back into the barrel of the shotgun, and put the others away in their containers.

Black Powder Rifles

Black Powder Rifles require cleaning within 12 hours of when they are fired. This is because of the corrosive effects of black powder. If even left over night after they have been shot, the black powder residue will begin to corrode the barrel and firing mechanism, hurting accuracy and consistency of firing. Much of the reputation black powder rifles have for misfiring is caused by improper cleaning, or not cleaning within 12 hours of firing. About 10 years ago, a friend of mine had a shot at a nice buck with his black powder rifle and it misfired. Back in camp while he was complaining and threatening to throw the rifle away, I examined his rifle. The firing mechanism was corroded. I asked him when he'd last cleaned it, and he admitted he hadn't cleaned it after he took it to the range a week earlier to sight it in.

Ordinary Windex window cleaner is the best product I've found to clean black powder guns. Use it on the same medium weight white cotton flannel that you use to clean other guns. Don't use any oils, oil-based solvents or any petroleum-based products on black powder guns because they won't effectively clean black powder residue and they mix with the black powder and create a gunk that's hard to remove. The Windex dries quickly and thoroughly and very effectively removes black powder residue. Bore Butter is a non-petroleum based grease that protects the metal from rusting and breech plug grease is a non-petroleum based grease that lubricates and seals the breech plug so gasses won't escape around it. These should always be used instead of petroleum-based products.

Disassemble the rifle according to the instructions in the owner's manual. Then, using cotton flannel patches soaked in Windex, wipe the black powder residue off the internal and external parts of the firing mechanism (striker mechanism or bolt mechanism, depending on the rifle) and any other places anywhere on the rifle or its parts that are stained black. If you have one of the newer break-open action types, there is no firing mechanism to clean, only the space under the chamber when the gun is broke open. Remove the breech plug using the breech plug wrench and wipe off the breech plug grease. Also thoroughly clean the breech plug threads inside the breech end of the barrel. You may also want to use an old tooth brush and q-tips to help. Push a small pick or piece of wire through the flash hole in the breech plug to make sure it's not obstructed.

Use a shotgun rod and tip with cotton flannel patches soaked in Windex to clean the bore. Push a Windex-soaked cotton flannel patch through the bore and discard the dirty patch. Then continue to push Windex-soaked patches through the bore until it's clean. It may take as many as six or eight patches. You shouldn't need to use a bronze bristle brush. Then push two or three dry patches through the bore to dry it out. Finally, lubricate a patch with Bore Butter, and push and pull it through the bore several times to protect the bore from rust.

Dry off all the parts you cleaned (the Windex dries quickly, so they may already be dry). Then spread breech plug grease liberally into the threads of the breech plug and screw it back into the breech with the breech plug wrench. Bore Butter won't work as breech plug grease because of the temperature the breech plug reaches, so be sure and use breech plug grease. Protect the exterior metal parts from rust by wiping them with a cloth that has a light coat of Bore Butter on it. Re-assemble the firing mechanism and attach the receiver and barrel to the stock.

The morning before you go on your first hunt, with the rifle unloaded, fire a 209 primer in the gun to make sure the flash hole is not obstructed. The rifle will not have to be cleaned after firing the 209 primer, only after firing black powder. If you do not shoot it, you can store the rifle loaded until the next hunt, but be sure it doesn't have a primer in it and be sure the muzzle is pointed in a safe direction. And if the house catches fire, get it out of the house quickly because the heat will make it shoot if it's got black powder in it.

If you do not shoot the rifle during the season, you don't have to shoot it to unload it. You can remove the breech plug and push the Pyrodex black powder pellets and the bullet out the breach end of the gun. Do not use these black powder pellets again. And clean the bore with Windex-soaked patches, dry it out and rust-protect it with a patch containing Bore Butter. Wipe the breech plug grease off the breech plug and the threads inside the breech end of the barrel, spread more breech plug grease into the threads of the breech plug and screw it back into the breech.

Resources

Solvents and Cleaners

EEZOX
Eezox Manufacturing
P.O. Box 1068
Solvang, CA 93464
Ph: 800-350-8999
www.eezox.info

Hoppe's No. 9 Solvent
Bushnell Outdoor Products
9200 Cody
Overland Park, KS 66214
Ph: 800-423-3537
www.hoppes.com

Rig
Silencio
56 Coney Island Dr.
Sparks, NV 89431
Ph: 800-648-1812
www.silencio.com

Rods

J. Dewey Manufacturing Co.
112 Willenbrock Rd.
Oxford, CT 06478
Ph: 203-264-3064
www.deweyrods.com

Flex Rods

Otis Technology, Inc.
6987 Laura St.
Lyons Falls, NY
Ph: 800-684-7486
www.otisgun.com

Brushes, Jags and Slotted Tips

Pro-Shot Products
311 S. Baughman Rd.
Taylorville, IL 62568
Ph: 217-824-9133
www.proshotproducts.com

Rifle Rests

MTM Molded Products Company
3370 Obco Court
Dayton, OH 45414
Ph: 937-890-7461
www.mtmcase-gard.com

Miscellaneous

Bass Pro Shops
Springfiled, MO
Ph: 800-494-1300
www.basspro.com for retail locations

Cabelas
Sidney, NE
Ph: 800-850-8402
www.cabelas.com for retail locations

Also By Robert Allen Morris

Available at www.amazon.com in paperback or on Kindle

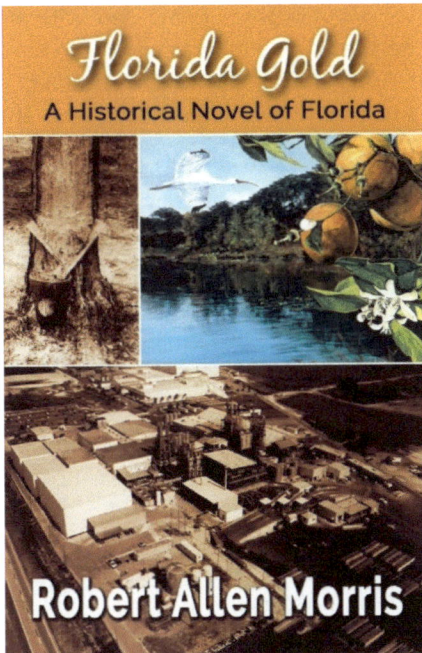

It's 1988, and Jack Thomas, the 73-year-old CEO of Tropical Juices, finally about to retire, reflects upon his life. The story quickly shifts back to Jack's birth in 1915 in a turpentine-making camp in rural Florida. The child of 15-year-old Irma Sue, who had been seduced by the son of a local moonshiner, Jack is to be raised as her brother by her parents, Pete and Margaret. Pete, however, is soon killed in a horse-riding accident. Irma Sue and Margaret move to Mobile, Alabama, hoping to earn enough money to bring Jack, left behind with friends, into a new home. Fortune smiles upon the attractive women, both marrying advantageously. The family reunites briefly before Jack is snatched to work the fields at one of Florida's illegal child labor camps. With the assistance of local Native Americans, Jack escapes from the camp as a teenager. He returns to Mobile, learns of further family catastrophe, then helps the feds bust up the camps. With seed money from a surprising source, Jack starts an orange-juice business in Florida, serves with distinction in World War II and continually expands his enterprise. By novel's end, he heads a multibillion-dollar company, although still more family losses make success bittersweet. Morris, an agricultural economist with over 30 years of experience in the citrus industry, brings plenty of insider knowledge and passion to this fictional work, managing to make sequences featuring the main character, Jack Thomas' savvy with concentrate, cartons that don't leak, and other innovations quite engaging. His narrative gets a bit overripe at times, given the seemingly never-ending and near-superhuman heroics of his main character as well as a rather melodramatic string of family tragedies. Still, this novel is ultimately highly entertaining, and a surprisingly juicy account about a key segment of commerce in the Sunshine State. --- *Kirkus Reviews*

Florida Gold by Robert Allen Morris was one of those 'wow factor' books. An amazingly told story, with real feeling put into the words. It's an unforgettable story, one that I could read over again and still take something new away from it. The characters are real and fit the story, the plot was well thought out and researched, and the whole book flows properly. Robert Morris is clearly a natural born storyteller and I would love to read more from him. – *Readers' Favorite*

Florida Gold was inducted into the Florida Citrus Archives on September 24, 2014. The event was hosted by the Lawton Chiles Center for Florida History on the Campus of Florida Southern College in Lakeland, Florida.

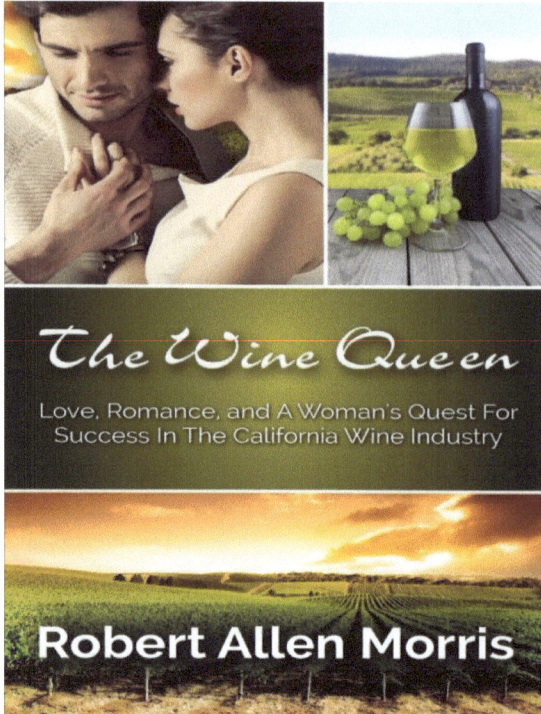

Ann Robinson is orphaned at the age of eight and sent to live with her Uncle Dave and mean-spirited, manipulative Aunt Harriett. Ann is smart, works hard in school, and goes to college. She graduates at the top of her class with a degree in economics, and accepts a job as a sales manager. When she sees Ray Collins presenting a paper at professional meetings, she becomes infatuated with him. But she learns that he's married with a family, although his marriage is troubled. Ann can't get Ray off of her mind, and ultimately decides that if she can't have Ray, then she'll never get married. She goes back to school, gets her master's degree, and climbs the corporate ladder at the Global Soft Drink Company. Ray's marriage finally ends, and when he and Ann go on their first date, they are powerfully attracted to each other. They subsequently fall deeply in love, have an incredibly romantic courtship, and get married. Ann is devastated when their marriage comes to an unexpected and abrupt end. She accepts a position as the chief financial officer for the Columbia Creek Winery, and moves to Napa, California. With the help of an equity investment from the Global Soft Drink Company, Ann buys the winery. She subsequently makes wines and develops new wine blends that become very popular and gain international recognition. Sales soar and she grows Columbia Creek Winery into the largest wine company in the world. But she never gives up on love and romance, as demonstrated by the surprising ending.

Reviewed by Valerie Rouse for Readers' Favorite

"The Wine Queen by Robert Allen Morris is a delightful story about a bright, educated young lady with good business acumen. It tells a tale about dedication. The main character, Ann Robinson, always committed herself to her goals and excelled. This is an admirable trait. Author Robert Morris did an excellent job developing the main character and displaying her inner strength and boldness. This feature is one which all readers should uphold. The tone is colloquial and quite easy to follow. I love the emphasis the author placed on the romance portion of the novel. This section was very intense emotionally and I was caught up in the rapture of the heated romance. I identified with Ann and felt that she deserved the attention and love being given. This indicates the creative genius of the author. I love the fact that the author chose to provide a little background on the upbringing of the main character. This allows the reader to understand her personality on a deeper level. The twist at the end was totally unexpected. It is not very realistic, but it is entertaining to read nevertheless. Overall, The Wine Queen is a good read, and I recommend it to all readers." ***Readers' Favorite***

About the Author

Robert Allen Morris, a Florida native, is an agricultural economist with over thirty years of experience in Florida agribusiness. He is currently Vice-President of Sales and Marketing for Blue Lake Citrus Products, Inc., the company that produces and markets the Noble brand of high end specialty citrus juices sold in supermarkets and restaurants, as well as bulk citrus juices sold to other brands and retail chains. From 2007 until 2012, Allen was on the faculty of the University of Florida in the Food and Resource Economics Department. His responsibilities included both educational programs and research. Prior to that, he held managerial positions with various agricultural, beverage, and financial services companies. Allen has been cleaning guns ever since he was eight years old and received his first .22 caliber rifle. There are guns in his safe that are less than three years old and many years old, guns that have been on many hunting trips and guns never shot. They all look equally new. And all of his rifles are 1.5 minute-of-angle accurate or better. He learned the procedures described in this book through experience, talking to manufacturers of gun cleaning equipment and materials, talking to gunsmiths, and research. Allen currently resides with his wife, Kate, in Florida, and can be contacted at AllenMors@aol.com. Visit www.AllenMorrisOnline.com for more literary works by Allen.

Notes

www.ingramcontent.com/pod-product-compliance
Lightning Source LLC
Chambersburg PA
CBHW041546040426
42447CB00002B/71